D0528373

Robin Hood

Retold by Rob Lloyd Jones

Illustrated by Alan Marks

Reading Consultant: Alison Kelly
Roehampton University

Contents

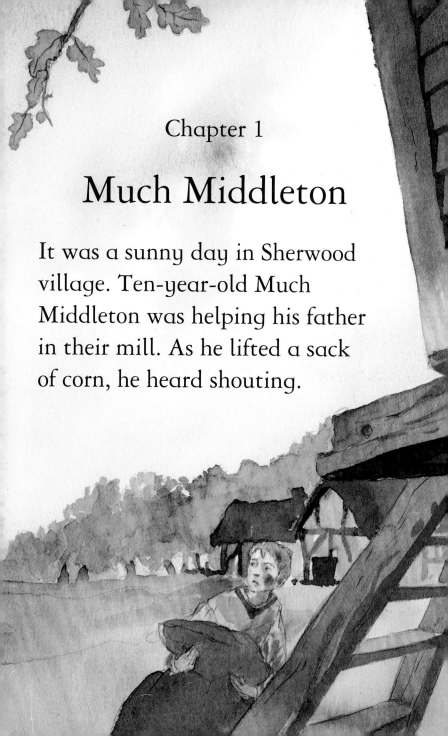

Chapter 1

Much Middleton

It was a sunny day in Sherwood village. Ten-year-old Much Middleton was helping his father in their mill. As he lifted a sack of corn, he heard shouting.

Dozens of soldiers pounded into the village on horseback, led by the Sheriff of Nottingham.

"I need more money," the Sheriff declared. He owned Sherwood and the villagers had to pay him taxes so they could live there.

From now on, you will all pay double.

Much's father was furious. "Only
the King is allowed to raise taxes,"
he protested.

The Sheriff sneered. "The King
is overseas. I'm in charge now."
With that, he lashed his horse and
charged back to his castle.

That evening, Much lay in bed watching his father count their money. There wasn't nearly enough. "Do you think Robin Hood could help us?" Much asked.

Robin Hood was a mysterious outlaw who stole money from the Sheriff to give to poor villagers. People said he lived in Sherwood Forest, though no one knew for sure.

Much was always asking for stories about Robin Hood. "Is it true he once defeated twenty of the Sheriff's men?"

"A hundred!" his father joked, waving a shovel.

Just then, there was a noise outside. Much's father gripped the shovel, scared it was the Sheriff's soldiers. He flung the door open...

...but no one was there. A silk pouch hung on the door, filled with twinkling gold coins.

Every house in the village had one.

"They're from Robin Hood," one of the villagers gasped.

"God bless him!" cried another.

"Much!" his father called. "Come quickly and see."

Robin Hood!

But Much had already seen. He sat by the window watching a shadowy figure leap across the rooftops to Sherwood Forest.

9

Chapter 2

On the run

The Sheriff was furious when he came back the next day. "Robin Hood stole that money from me," he spat.

Much hated the Sheriff. In a rage, he scooped up some horse dung...

...and hurled it splat into the Sheriff's face. "God bless Robin Hood!" he shouted.

Several guards tried to grab Much, but his father blocked their way. They forced his father to the ground. "Run!" he yelled to Much.

Much fled into the forest and scrambled up a tree to hide. His heart was pounding. Tears trickled down his cheeks. His father had been arrested, and it was all his fault.

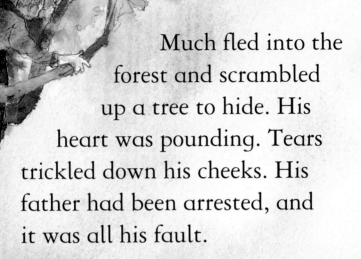

Much was desperate to rescue him, but how? He needed help. He needed to find Robin Hood.

Chapter 3

Sherwood Forest

Much wandered deeper into the forest. The trees seemed to close in around him. He was tired, thirsty and scared.

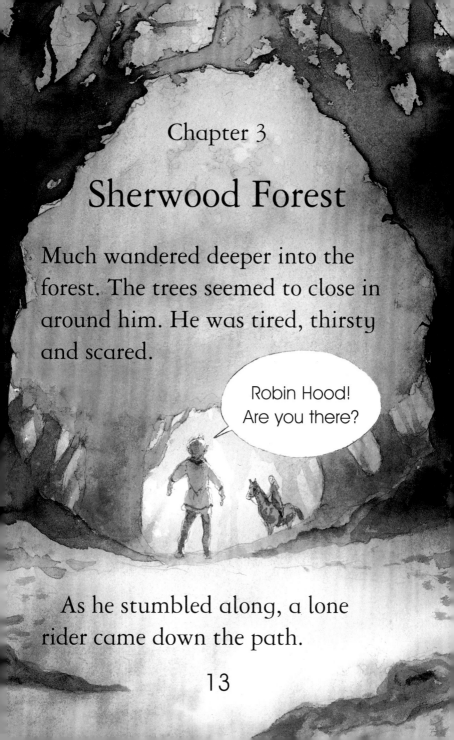

Robin Hood! Are you there?

As he stumbled along, a lone rider came down the path.

13

It was a woman, wearing a silk dress and a glittering necklace.

Can I give you a ride?

Much recognized her at once – Lady Marian, the King's cousin.

"Jump up behind me," she said. "Where are you going?"

Much was exhausted. "I don't
know," he mumbled, as he climbed
onto Marian's horse.

Just then, Marian saw something
in the trees. "Outlaws!" she cried.
"Hold on tight!" She grasped the
reins and they raced down the path.

Much looked up. High in the forest, several figures were leaping from tree to tree, shadowing them.

They reached a crossroads and Marian stopped the horse. "They've gone," she sighed with relief.

But she didn't see the figure
reaching out behind them...

Marian screamed. Her necklace
had been stolen!

Much jumped from the horse and raced into the woods. "Are you there Robin Hood?" he shouted. "I need your help."

All he saw were the branches, rustling in the wind.

"They've gone, and taken my necklace with them," said Marian, catching up with him.

"ROBIN HOOD!" Much yelled.

At his cry, four dark figures appeared among the branches.

"You'd better come with us," one ordered. "Follow the arrows."

Thunk! An arrow thudded into the path in front of Much.

Much climbed up behind Marian
again and they followed one arrow...

then another...

then several more.

They jumped over bushes and rode
under branches, until they reached a
clearing in the heart of the forest.

Several small houses sat hidden among a circle of trees. A tangled net of branches disguised them from anyone who might pass.

Three men greeted them
with friendly smiles.
"Are you Robin Hood?"
Much asked the largest one.

"No," said the
man, scratching
his bushy beard.
"I'm Little John."

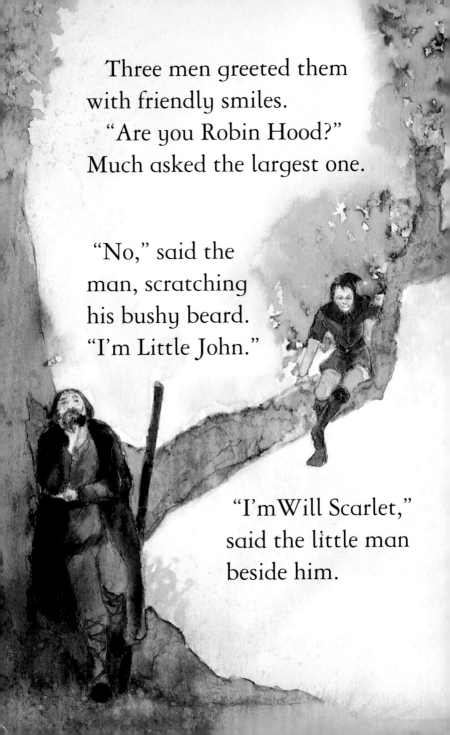

"I'm Will Scarlet,"
said the little man
beside him.

"And I'm Friar Tuck," said the third man, who wore a long monk's robe.

"Is Robin Hood even here?" asked Much, in frustration.

"Right here," a voice replied. The famous outlaw was leaning against a tree, grasping a longbow.

"Thanks for the necklace," he said.

Marian strode forward angrily. "That necklace was a gift from my uncle," she fumed. "Why would *you* want it?"

"He won't keep it," Much explained. "He gives all his loot to the villagers."

"Really?" Marian asked, surprised. Robin nodded, then offered Marian her necklace back.

"In that case," Marian said, "keep it. I thought you were just a common thief."

"No," said Robin, winking at Much, "I'm a very good thief."

"We were farmers once," Robin explained, "but the Sheriff stole our land. Now, we help the villagers keep theirs."

"Can you help my father?" Much asked. "I think he's been locked in the Sheriff's dungeons."

Robin shook his head, then turned to go. "I'm sorry," he said, "that's too dangerous. The King will free him when he returns. Until then, you can live with us."

But Much was determined to rescue his father – with or without Robin Hood.

Chapter 4

Robin and Much

That night, Much stole one of the outlaw's swords and crept out of the clearing.

"Leaving already?" a voice called. Robin stepped from the shadows.

"I'm going to rescue my father," Much snapped, "because you won't."

Robin took the sword away from Much and put it down. "Come with me," he said.

Robin guided Much through the trees. They jumped from branch to branch, and swung together on tangled vines. Soon, they reached Sherwood village.

Robin handed Much a jingling pouch of coins. "Here," he said, "help me hand these out."

They split up and crept around
the village, crawling across
rooftops and slipping between
houses to leave the money.

Much left coins on villagers' doorsteps…

on their windowsills…

…and even under their pillows. He was on a thrilling secret mission – but he couldn't forget his father.

When the money was all gone, Robin sat down beside Much.

"This is why we can't try to rescue your father," said Robin. "If we get caught, how will the villagers pay their taxes?"

Much knew Robin was right. He glared at the Sheriff's castle. "Then, until my father is free, I'll help you protect the villagers," he promised.

The next day, Friar Tuck cooked
a huge lunch for the gang in the
forest – roast deer, rabbit stew and
blackberry pie.

Afterwards, Little John and
Will Scarlet taught Much how to
fight with a sword.

And Robin
trained him
in archery.

With each arrow,
Much got closer to
the bulls-eye...

THWACK!

THWACK!

THWACK!

...but he was
never as good
as Robin Hood.

Much spent weeks living with Robin and his men. He helped them steal from the rich...

...and give to the poor.

He invented clever disguises...

sneaky hiding places...

Thanks for the money! Robin Hood

...and mocking messages for the greedy Sheriff.

Much loved being part of Robin Hood's gang. But he still worried about his father, locked up in the Sheriff's castle.

Chapter 5

The Sheriff's castle

One morning, Lady Marian visited
the Sheriff. She wondered if he had
any news of her cousin. The King
had been due home weeks before.

"My dear," the Sheriff said, "I'm afraid he is probably dead."

"And you want to replace him," Marian realized with horror.

"Who else?" boasted the Sheriff. "I'm the richest man in the country."

"You're a crook," Marian cried. "Robin Hood will stop you."

The Sheriff just sneered at the outlaw's name. "I don't think so."

The Sheriff took Marian to the
next room. Six knights stood by the
fire, all dressed in black. They had
snake-like eyes and brutal faces.

"The Six Swordsmen," Marian
gasped.

The Six Swordsmen were the
most feared fighters in Europe.

"They're my new tax collectors," the Sheriff said proudly. "I'd like to see Robin Hood stop them."

But Marian had already gone.

Chapter 6

The Swordsmen strike

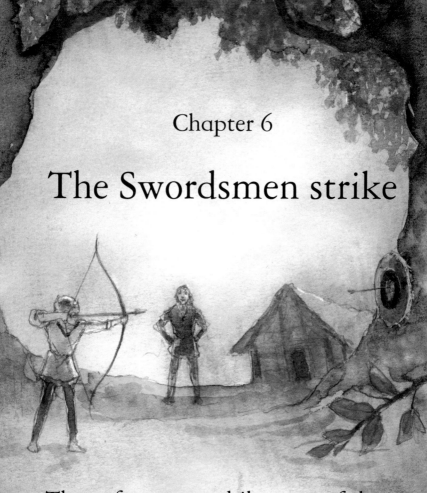

That afternoon, while some of the outlaws took more money to the village, Robin gave Much another archery lesson. As Much pulled back his bow...

...Marian came charging into the clearing.

"Robin!" she called. "The Sheriff has hired the Six Swordsmen."

Just then, a plume of smoke rose in the sky.

"It's coming from the village!" cried Robin, grabbing his sword.

Much couldn't believe his eyes when they reached the village. All of the houses had been burned down, including his father's mill. The villagers wandered forlornly through the ruins.

"It was the Six Swordsmen," one said. "We gave them money, but they still destroyed our homes."

"Where are Will and Tuck and Little John?" demanded Robin.

"Captured," the villager said sadly. "The Swordsmen took them to the castle."

Robin stared up at the Sheriff's castle, his face darkening. "It's time to fight back," he declared.

"But how?" asked Marian. "The Sheriff has a whole army."

Much scrambled onto the remains of the mill and called to the villagers. "Will you join us? Will you join Robin Hood?"

Much grinned. Now they had an army too.

Chapter 7

To the castle

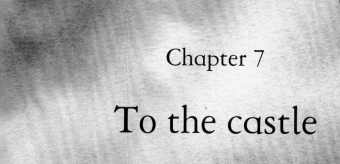

In the dead of night, an arrow shot
into the air. A trail of rope uncoiled
from the end as it stuck high in the
wall of the Sheriff's castle.

Among the trees, Robin pulled the rope tight. "Are you sure you're ready?" he asked Much.

Much nodded. He'd never been more sure of anything.

Below, Marian and the villagers watched in silence as the pair climbed the rope to the castle.

The rope dug into Much's hands. He tried not to look down. Soon, Robin was pulling him onto the moonlit castle walkway. Everything was deadly quiet...

...until a door crashed open and the Six Swordsmen emerged.

"Robin Hood," one growled. "We've been expecting you."

Chapter 8

Fight!

The Swordsmen charged. They were so fast, Much could hardly see their swords. But Robin was faster.

50

The outlaw twisted and twirled, ducked and dived. He drove the Swordsmen down a spiral staircase into the main hall.

Much pushed hard against a statue of the Sheriff, toppling it onto four of the Swordsmen. But there were still two left.

They lunged at Much,
whirling their swords.

Much darted across the floor, but
he was trapped. The Swordsmen
advanced, grinning evilly. Quickly,
Robin scrambled up a pillar.

Then he leaped from the
balcony…

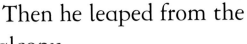

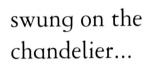

swung on the
chandelier…

…and crashed into the last two
Swordsmen, sending them flying.

"Come on!" he urged Much. "We
must find the prisoners."

But before they could move,
dozens of soldiers had surrounded
them, blocking the way.

The Sheriff stood by with a smug
smile. "There are too many
of us," he scoffed. "Even for you."

Much spun and fired a single arrow. It whizzed over their heads and through the castle entrance.

At his signal, Marian and the villagers stormed inside. A huge battle began.

As the battle raged, Marian led Much down some stairs to the dungeons. There sat his father, locked in chains, alongside Little John, Will Scarlet and Friar Tuck.

They grabbed the keys from a hook and released the prisoners. Much's father scooped him up in a big hug.

When they returned to the main hall, the fight was over. Only the Sheriff refused to surrender.

"You can't stop me," he snarled. "The King is dead!"

"Really?" a voice roared from the castle entrance. "I feel quite alive."

The King strode into the hall.
Marian threw her arms around
him. "You're back!" she cried.

The Sheriff gave a squeal of
panic, turned and ran.

As he passed, Much stuck out
a leg. The Sheriff fell screaming
down the stairs to the dungeon.

Little John slammed the door,
and Will Scarlet turned the key.
Then they raced up the stairs and
bowed to the King.

"I owe you a huge debt," the King told Robin and his men. "I'll make you all knights. You can live together in this castle."

"Thank you sir," Robin said, "but the forest is our home."

"You can stay with us if you like," Robin added to Much.

Much shook his head. "My home is the village," he replied, hugging his father.

Robin handed Much his sword. "Keep this then, to remember us."

With that, Robin Hood and his men were gone.

"Do you think we'll ever see them again?" Much asked.

"I'm sure we will," the King replied, "if we need their help."

And so, Much Middleton's life returned to normal. The King had all of the villagers' homes rebuilt, including the mill, and Much went back to working with his father.

One thing was different, though – now Much's father asked *him* for stories about Robin Hood.

About the story

No one really knows if Robin Hood ever existed,
although there was a Sheriff of Nottingham during
the Middle Ages, and a huge forest in Sherwood.
Outlaws lived there in secret hideouts. Some
became popular heroes, because they fought back
against corrupt officials. Villagers told stories
about an outlaw they called Robin Hood.
These stories became legend.

Series editor: Lesley Sims
Designed by Michelle Lawrence

First published in 2008 by Usborne Publishing Ltd.,
83-85 Saffron Hill, London EC1N 8RT, England.
www.usborne.com
Copyright © 2008 Usborne Publishing Ltd.

All rights reserved. No part of this publication may be reproduced,
stored in a retrieval system or transmitted in any form or by any
means, electronic, mechanical, photocopying, recording or otherwise
without the prior permission of the publisher. The name Usborne
and the devices ♀ ⊕ are Trade Marks of Usborne Publishing Ltd.
Printed in China. UE. First published in America in 2008.